Strategies for Start Up Businesses

ISBN-13: 978-1983476297

ISBN-10: 1983476293

Copyright © 2017 by Diane Winbush

Cover image Illustration *by Mauricio Feldman-Abe*

Day One

Prepare to Start

On Your Mark Get Ready, Set, Go! Preparation begins within the goals of your vision. Getting a clear thought process of how you desire your business or career to be structured. Search out the what, when, where, why, and how of your vision and or mission strategy.

Day Two

Plan

Select long & short-term goals for your career and business. Plan strategically to meet those goals.
Write them down and mark them off as you accomplish the goals. The short-term goals should maneuver into the long-term goals.

Day Three

Financially Fit

Keep a financial tracking sheet such as a budget spreadsheet of all credits and debits expenses the business incurs while in business.

Spending without a track sheet can spell disaster. which includes; spending on demand verses spending on the shelf.

A business or career will not meet its obligations if it purchases items which are not immediate demand.

For example: Kristie has a flower shop and opened it three weeks; she only has three clients and she has purchased a new vehicle to transport flowers for or three clients.

 This is not a demand. Wait until your clientele builds.

Day Four

Make it Happen

A train will never move unless you apply the petroleum, the keys, and someone to drive.
You are the driver of your business and career.
Procrastination will never get anything accomplished

Day Five

Willing to Accept Challenges

Getting your career & business off for marketing & branding can present some challenges.
Learn how to listen to others whom may provide constructive criticism to you in areas which need attention.

For example, Mark has written a novel which is ready for publishing.
The manuscript needs to go through one last stage. The stage is proofreading and then feedback.

It's like producing a movie and it is shown to its critics before it hits the box office.

Critics will share their opinions to the public and the producers of what they feel that will be successful and that which they feel will fail the box office.

Listening to others whether you agree or disagree is very helpful.

Accept, thank your critics, and move forward.

Day Six

Never Be Afraid to ask for Help

Seeking a mentor for business tips, tools, and resources is a great strategic move.

There are many organizations; such as S.C.O.R.E (free tool) will be happy to support you.

Each area has their own chapter. Go to *www.s.c.o.r.e.com*. You can also join organizations which are on Facebook and seek mentors from this platform. There are also paid groups which can support your endeavor such as the *American Marketing Association* and Public Relations Society of America.

Day Seven

Be a Listener

Never be the aardvark, as if you know everything. People care less about your certificates, awards, training, and accolades.
They want to know can you listen. A good listener will always gain everything else which some cannot.

Day Eight
Communication

This is critical. For example; Sharon has a Facebook Ad page.
She and her team has launched the page, created a budget for it, and now it's ready for release.
Sharon selects all the right demographics for the campaign.

After the campaign has completed; she has a low response rate.
Sharon has pitched the perfect ad, but no one noticed it. This is because Sharon doesn't interact with others regarding her business.
She is isolated on her Facebook accounts. She never interacts with others in her community of her brand.

But Sharon expects that her campaign will be successful. After all; Sharon and her team has pitched a $5,000.00 budget for this campaign. Communicating with others can really boost your sales for business.

All the time, the conversation doesn't have to be about you or your brand. Just communicate. Just your conversation can become so compelling, that others will know that you are a professional product.

Day Nine

Networking

Engaging with local events is a sure way of building your business for success.
There may be the perfect fit and targeted entrepreneur present for your business.

Be willing to network with others for great ideas and other events which are upcoming in the area. You can't build a business all by yourself.

You will need others to connect with to share your story, brand, and or product. We need each other to excel.

Donna needs people to launch the new high energy drink she created. Attending networks around your city will help to get the word out of your business.

Day Ten

Fresh Credentials

Always monitor your business cards and information to see if something has changed. This includes your business address, phone number, email, and or website.

Your media kit should always remain updated. Attendants for a workshop frowns on rubbed out information with pens and markers.

Day Eleven

Becoming More Acclimated for Business

Always become more acclimated with your business by searching for more creative ways for advancement and growth. Remember; you are the major key player for the business.

Research what makes your brand stand out from your competitors.

Learn how your brand can add value to others.

Day Twelve

Market your Business

There are tons of ways to market your business. While social media tends to grow rapidly; this will be a great opportunity to advertise and market. Another marketing strategy is to wear your brand on you.

Many developers and entrepreneurs will wear monogrammed shirts of their logos to advertise their business.

Market your business in local newspapers and publications.

Creating a blog account will help your customers and clients to remain consistent with your product and business.

Blogging will compel visitors to your website. Subscribers list will intrigue customers to find out more about you.

Creating a website will show your brand off.

Creating a Google AdSense campaign to review your analytics will help you to see how well your business is doing.

Day Thirteen

Wealth Overnight?

Never get caught up in get rich quick schemes Always be willing to face adversity or setbacks head on. Remember you are in business to build a foundation and platform for success.

Seeking microwave wealth and no hard work put in, will surely set you up for failure. When you have built your company, and can appreciate how far you've come; you've put in "sweat-equity." Investinganswers.com states it like this; *"Sweat equity is used to describe the non-financial investment that people contribute to the development of a project such as a start-up business.*

For example, sweat equity is counted from the founders of the company, as well as advisors and board members."

Day Fourteen

Advertising

Get your business in front of millions with local television, social media platforms, and more.

If one entity isn't working; move to the next strategy. If you sit and wait for a response from one entity; you will become stagnated. I have learned that you must spend money to get money. Move around!

Day Fifteen

Get Feedback

Always ask your clients for feedback or have survey sheets at your events and conferences.

You can also create a survey campaign and offer your customers an incentive for taking the survey.

If your business is in retail; you can have a link on the printed receipt for the customer to access on their smartphone.
  This will help you to know how to be more creative for success and how you can improve.

There are also online surveys software such as *SurveyMonkey, Qualtrics,* just to name a few.

Day Sixteen

Accept Failure

Always be willing to accept failure. You cannot have success without some mistakes and lessons learned in business.
If you are always riding high in the clouds; you will eventually come down to see your issues.

Failures only hurt for a season not for a lifetime.

Day Seventeen

Accept Criticism

There will be times when someone whom you may not be acquainted with will tap you on the shoulder and provide some do's and don'ts regarding your business.

Be willing to accept the information to strive for perfection.

Day Eighteen

Avoid Social Media Bashing

Remember a potential client may view your conduct and refuse to do business with you due to your conduct of bashing others for business. There is no competition in your business if you have a solid foundation. No worries!

Day Nineteen

Professional Attire

Attires are important! It's your second business card. It says a lot about you and to your clients. For example: Sherri attended a *Sun Trust Bank* conference with sandals and a skirt.

Sherri should have had a professional blouse, skirt, and pump heeled shoes. Dress accordingly to the event and purpose of the event.

Potential clients will write you off according to how you present yourself.

Day Twenty

Get it in Writing

An old saying goes; "business is business." Business should be conducted in a conservative manner.

For example; Paul has contacted Jim; a hardware store owner.

Paul and Jim speak about a business venture as a stakeholder in the company.

This will bring value to both business owners.
Jim has promised Paul that he has his okay om this business deal and that he has agreed to the terms and conditions.

But the business was never completed, because it was word of mouth.

The closeout date is within seven days and Jim hasn't notified Paul of his decision. Jim has run into a personal issue and forgot to mention this to Paul. Max; an executive for a high-ranking department store wants to become a stakeholder in the business.

Max has the revenue to become registered and a member immediately. Paul is reminded of himself; that he promised Jim the seat of this stakeholders' position.

But Max is willing to increase the value of what Paul offered Jim. Paul excepts the offer from Max. Jim returns to his CMO (Chief Marketing Officer) and they agree to the deal. Jim returns a week later; ready and prepared to sign.

But the stakeholders' opportunity has been given to Max. Jim is furious and questions Pauls' decision in this.

Paul advised Jim that he never heard a reply from him and that he gave the opportunity to another potential client. The moral of this scenario is that; if Jim was truly interested; he could've gotten Paul to agree to a written agreement, so that their agreement and terms were binding. Never do business without a pen and paper.

It can save future legalities. As a publisher and CEO; I always make sure that I get a signature from clients which has promised me business or that I have agreed to work with them in a business deal. Peoples' decision may change, and you're left out in the cold. They are to sign on the dotted line.

Day Twenty-One

Giving Back

Just as there were those whom supported you up the ladder of success;
always be willing to give back to others through free resources and tools such as conferences video conferencing, and webinars.

Day Twenty-Two

Appreciation

Those two words of thank you can take your character a long way.

Clients appreciate you more when you thank them for their support.

Remember you were seeking for them when you found them.

Day Twenty-Three

Going Free

When starting a business, most to all your resources and tools can be free. It's just a matter of searching.

Most of your business training can be obtained on online free courses, mentors, conferences, libraries, and webinars. You can train yourself until you can become more financially stable. There are also paid resources which are under $25.00. *Lynda.com*, which is a LinkedIn resource and *Udemy.com* are two powerful resources which can catapult your knowledge and business. *Lynda.com* can be free if you register through your local library with your library card.

Day Twenty-Four

Accountability

I'm the boss! But, being your boss doesn't exempt you from holding yourself accountable.

Holding yourself, staff member, or volunteers accountable for un-necessary issues that arose due to their negligence;

will uphold your business in the future.

For example: If someone left the memo note pads for your event at the office, meet up, or consultation; who are you going to hold accountable for the error?

An issue will continue to exist unless the matter is rectified.

Day Twenty-Five

Responsibility

Always take ownership for your actions and don't gripe behind it. This shows a sign of maturity.
If you complain about everything then you will be toxic for the business. be responsible. Don't shift the blame.

Day Twenty-Six

Customer Service

As an entrepreneur, coach, or ceo; you are going to be the first voice a customer or client hears.

Making sure that you have appropriate courtesy and speech etiquette is essential for growth.

Why? Your opening response will tell your client if you are worth the time.

Day Twenty-Seven

Overly Suspicious

It is one thing to be watchful and cautious of potential clients whom desire to take you for a ride.

But we must remain neutral that we don't become overly suspicious. Everyone don't have a desire to mimic you for business. If you've seen it before; you should know how to react.

Day Twenty-Eight

Growth for Business

Always search out ways for more growth and visibility. You can achieve higher when you shoot for the stars.
The stars are within you and how far you feel you can reach them. Take your bow and arrow and aim for your target for growth

Day Twenty-Nine
Support Charities

Potential customers are compelled to new businesses and matured companies when they give back to special causes and charities.

As Entrepreneurs and career developers; we are always taking; such as fees for events and online tutorials.

Giving back to local and national charities will allow other companies to recognize your business as a giver and not always a taker. We must drop the selfish mechanism.

Day Thirty

Resolutions

There will be times which you will need to make some tough decisions even if they are due to conflict.

A leader; such as an entrepreneur, will always have clear, correct, and concise decisions.

Never brush-off a customer/consumer because you don't have the answer or fail to rectify the issue. Remember, as a business owner/ you are a problem solver to your own product and brand.

If a consumer can't refer to you, who can they refer too. Make good resolutions for the business.

Make a list of some *what-ifs* for the business. Always think a step ahead for the consumer.

Day Thirty-One

Walk the Walk

We must be able to take in what we dish out! If you can instruct someone else; you must also be willing for others to instruct you. This will bring more strong leadership and maturity on your part.

This also refers to tardiness of meetings, absenteeism of events, cancellations of meet ups, etc.

Summary

Starting a business will lead to a wall of success when you follow strategic steps and remain consistent with what you begin for the consumer.

There will be failures and many opportunities when building your brand and product. Learning how to make the most from your critics will lead your business to a five-star rating.

www.ingramcontent.com/pod-product-compliance
Lightning Source LLC
Chambersburg PA
CBHW040231220526
45473CB00001B/195